Into the Wilds:
A Mothers Guide to Wilderness Therapy

Copyright © 2022 by Michelle King

All rights reserved.

No part of this book may be reproduced in any form or by any electronic or mechanic means, including information storage and retrieval systems, without written permission from the author, except for brief quotations in a book review.

International Standard Book Number: 9798829988326

The content of this book is for informational purposes only and is not intended to diagnosis, treat, cure or prevent any conditions. The authors make no guarantees concerning the level of success you may experience with wilderness therapy treatment.

Drew and Lucy

Without you, this book would not have been possible. You are both loved so much, and we are forever thankful for your growth and the wonderful young adults you've both become. We are also grateful for what we have learned about ourselves and who we have become as a result of your journey.

TABLE OF CONTENTS

Introduction - 1
What is happening to my family? - 3
Who is eligible for Wilderness Therapy? - 5
How to choose a program - 8
Paying for treatment is not easy -14
Myths and other concerns - 18
Why Wilderness Therapy? - 23
Getting to the woods - 29
What is my role now? -38
A day in the woods - 43
From F-you to thank you - 53
Graduating from wilderness - 61
The home contract - 67
Importance of aftercare - 71
Wrap up - 74
Drews story - 75
Lucys story - 78
Scotts story - 82
Marks story - 86
Sample contract - 90
Resources - 94
Citations - 97
Acknowledgments - 99

INTRODUCTION

"A week in the wilderness is like a month at a residential."

Our names are Michelle and Jenny and both of us made the agonizing decision to send our then 16-year children to a wilderness therapy program. Coming to that decision was not easy and we had our doubts and concerns, but we were both at the point where we did not know what else to try.

Our kids went to the same wilderness therapy program and amazingly ended up in the same aftercare program. We met in the aftercare parent support group. In getting to know each other we realized that we both had a passion for sharing our stories. Wilderness therapy is often misunderstood and thought of as a drastic and harsh option, but since it was so beneficial to our kids and our families we wanted to get some basic knowledge regarding this option out to others. While there is so much information that we could share regarding Wilderness therapy we know that your life is probably pretty crazy and hectic right now and you are at your wit's end as to what your next step should be, therefore, we decided to keep this book quite simple and straightforward. Please know that we are only scratching the surface of all that is Wilderness Therapy.

Our children and their journeys could not have been more different, yet both ended up in a wilderness therapy program and benefited greatly from their time there. Drew went due to anger issues and Lucy went due to drug use. Drew went willingly and Lucy was "gooned" – meaning she did not go willingly. One family hired an education consultant, the other did not. Drew came home after his stay in wilderness while Lucy went to a therapeutic boarding school after her discharge. So, despite two vastly different stories, the end results were the same, and that was both teens had their lives changed for the better due to their time in wilderness therapy. We each spoke to our kids who participated in the program, and both felt it was a fantastic idea and they fully supported our decision to share their stories.

We were truly fortunate that we were able to find a program that helped heal not only our children but our families. Please understand that not all programs are created equally, like all things in life some programs are not as helpful and could even be harmful. While this treatment worked for us, it is not a guarantee that it will be successful for all who attend. The majority of the following information included comes directly from our children's experiences at the wilderness therapy program we choose for them. We were able to speak to several other teens who went to different programs and their stories and experiences are touched upon in the following pages.

WHAT IS HAPPENING TO MY FAMILY?

If you are reading this then you are probably in a battle right now. A battle with a teenager, while wondering, where did I go wrong? Who is this teenager living in my home? What are we going to do with them? Will life ever go back to normal? Can I love them enough to get them through this? If you have been asking yourself these questions, then I have no doubt that this book will resonate with you. We, the moms that drafted this book, met because our teens were in treatment together. We became fast friends—the kind of friends that cast no judgment, but only offer love, support, and hope through a desperate situation. This book and our stories are here to help you navigate through one potential treatment option and to give you hope. There is hope that you have not lost your teen, hope that life can return to a new and beautiful normal, and the acceptance and reassurance that you did not cause this, nor did you do anything wrong in raising your teen.

I can remember years ago, when my teen was a cute cuddly 2-year-old, I met a wilderness therapist. As he explained wilderness therapy to me, my first thought was "Who'd ever send their kids to live in the woods for weeks on end – that's horrible?!" Little did I know that 14 years later I would be that parent. It is a tough decision to make; a decision usually made within days of realizing something needs to be done NOW. We are here to share our experiences with you and help you understand what wilderness therapy is and how it works. Our desire is to give you hope and reassurance that wilderness therapy can be an excellent option.

Please keep in mind that we are NOT doctors, therapists, counselors, or even writers. We are simply moms who realized that we, and our teen, needed help. We are moms who knew absolutely nothing about wilderness therapy, but who learned along the way. And now, most importantly, we are moms who are here to support you in your journey.

WHO IS ELIGIBLE FOR WILDERNESS THERAPY?

As a parent looking for treatments, you may be wondering whether wilderness therapy would be a good option for your teen. Surprisingly, there is a vast array of disorders and addictions that can be treated utilizing wilderness therapy. If you are unsure if your teen meets the criteria for wilderness therapy, consider reaching out to different programs and speaking with the staff. We found they were willing to talk with us and provide guidance to help sort out potential treatment options for our teen. We say teen but know that some programs will accept kids as young as 10 years of age. Below is a list of just some of the potential diagnoses that have been successfully treated in the woods.

**Behavioral and Mental Health disorders

-ADHD (Attention Deficit Hyperactivity disorder)

-ODD (Oppositional defiant disorder)

-Depression/Anxiety/Bi-polar disorder

-PTSD (Post traumatic stress disorder)

-Low self esteem

-Conflicts within the family unit

-Anger

-Lack of social and communication skills

**Addiction

-Alcohol

- Prescription Drugs

-Marijuana and synthetic marijuana

-Street and Club drugs

-Video game and technology

**Other

-Autism/Aspergers

-Identity Issues

-Gender Dysphoria

-Grief and loss

- Sexually acting out
- Victims of abuse
- Self entitlement

While the above list is quite inclusive, there are a few situations in which a child may not be considered appropriate for a wilderness program. Any child with a diagnosis of psychosis may not be eligible due to safety concerns. Teens with a history of sexual assault could also be excluded. If the child is cognitively low functioning their admittance would need to be addressed to determine if they would be able to participate in and understand the program. Lastly, those with physical limitations, such as being wheelchair-bound or needing intensive medical care would also need to be pre-screened by the facility. Once again, we recommend reaching out to facilities to see if they admit children with the diagnosis with which you are dealing.

HOW TO CHOOSE A PROGRAM

Once the decision has been made that it is time for a different path, you will probably feel very overwhelmed as you start looking at various options. Some families will research programs themselves while others may hire an education consultant to help navigate all the available options. I began my search with a "wilderness therapy near me" google search – and I had my child in a program a week later. I have since discovered several online groups that focus on wilderness therapy, and they are a wealth of knowledge. These groups have information on education consultants, different programs, post wilderness options, financial assistance, and anything else you may want to know. I have been truly shocked as I have learned more about wilderness therapy and just how many programs there are all over the United States. The web page "Find Child & Youth Residential Treatment" is a great place to start your search

(check kele for programs)

(childresidentialtreatment.com). This site breaks down facilities by state and briefly discusses each facilities target clientele, treatment model as well as cost. If you choose to hire an education consultant they will review your childs and family history and help you with the search for the appropriate placement. When it is time to start making phone calls to the programs you may not be sure what questions to ask or what to even look for in a program. Below are some questions that parents have found helpful when researching programs:

**Is the program licensed or accredited? How long have they had the license? Are they accredited by a mental health agency? Have they had any violations? Check out these web pages for the organizations below:

-Commission on Accreditation of Rehabilitation Facilities (CARF)

-Outdoor Behavioral Healthcare Council (OBHC)

**Are there licensed clinicians working with your teen?

**Is there a medical doctor or Psychiatrist on staff?

**Does the program offer school credits?

**What is the therapeutic model they use?

-several options are CBT (cognitive behavioral therapy), EMDR (eye movement desensitization & reprocessing), attachment therapy, CPT (cognitive processing therapy), DBT (dialectical behavior therapy).

**What is the level of family involvement and communication?

**Is there a spiritual or religious component to the program?

-we choose a nonreligious program yet when my son asked for a Bible they immediately provided one for him.

**What is the background of the owners?

**How do you find and hire staff? What does your staff retention look like?

**What are the ages of the other kids who will be with my child?

**Can my child be on their medications? How are they stored and who will administer them?

**What measures do you have in place to ensure my child's safety? How do you handle medical emergencies?

**Does the program specialize in any particular diagnosis? Do they have experience working with kids that have diagnosis similar to your child?

**What is the breakdown of time my child will be in the woods versus at base camp?

-Nomadic: The kids will spend the majority of their stay in the wilderness and will only go back to base camp on an infrequent basis. The therapist will come out to the field to meet with the kids for their sessions and will also bring new food supplies at this time.

-Base Camp/Hybrid: In this model the kids will return to base camp weekly or on a scheduled basis for showers, to replenish supplies, and meet with their therapist.

-Adventure therapy: The kids will have adventure obstacles that they must complete such as rope courses, rappelling, or rafting.

prefer a move to this over adventure rly

Each family will have different thoughts and opinions on what they find important in choosing a program. For example, for our family, we were not concerned with whether the program offered school credit. We decided that it would be ok if our son had to repeat a year of school, so the fact that the program we choose did not offer schooling was OK with us. Also, some programs are a better fit for certain diagnoses and circumstances, so when you are checking out programs make sure that you are open and honest regarding your situation. Family, friends, and even complete strangers will often voice strong opinions on what they feel the best options are regarding where to send your child and what you should deem important. They may even try to discourage you from utilizing a wilderness therapy program. We feel that you need to remember that you are the parent, and you know what is best for your child and your family, therefore, do what you feel is best for your individual situation.

We were able to connect with a staff member at a wilderness therapy program and we asked her for tips on how to vet a program. She recommended asking the facilities for names and numbers of past clients and reaching out to them for reviews on the program. My initial thought in obtaining recommendations was to pay more attention to the parent's reviews versus the child's. The above staff member feels like the child's review is a greater source of information than the parents. If the child had a positive experience they will be open and honest with their review and give examples of why the program was a success for them. If a teen takes the time to write a positive review then the program was pretty meaningful to them. Many parents do not write a positive review about their experience, even if it was a wonderful one. They often carry guilt and/or embarrassment, as well as want to protect their children from people knowing they were in treatment. Focusing just on internet reviews can lead you to conclude that wilderness therapy is the worse thing you could ever put your child through; that you will be causing even greater damage to them. Usually, people will complain and write a negative review before giving a compliment and writing a positive one. Please keep that in mind when reading these reviews. We also recommend when reading reviews that you check the date the review was written, as what you are reading could be several years old. Lastly, if the program is privately owned you should research the background of the owners. While the program may be just starting and not have much of a history to review, the owners may have been in the business for years with a wealth of knowledge. The National Association of Therapeutic Schools and Programs website (natsap.org) has a parent section that offers information as to questions to ask when researching a program as well as financial options and assistance with finding a program. If during your research you discover that the facility has any violations then ask them about the situation. Can they adequately and openly explain what happened and how they handled the situation?

When hiring an educational consultant to assist in finding the right program, consider the following questions before signing on with them:

**Do you accept any compensation from the facilities you refer to? (The answer should be NO)

**Do you guarantee admittance? (Once again the answer should be NO)

**What is your background and why/how did you get into this field?

**Discuss all fees upfront. Find out what services they will provide for you as well as how long the contract time will be.

**Will they assist with just a wilderness placement or will they also help with post wilderness placement and transition?

Once again, please keep in mind that not all programs are the same. We carefully read all the reviews we could find on the various programs looking for red flags. It is not easy to weigh the good reviews with the bad ones, but it is an important and necessary step in the process.

PAYING FOR TREATMENT IS NOT EASY

When you first start exploring the option of wilderness therapy there is a good chance you will be shocked at the expense. It is not cheap. The next question is, where do we get this kind of cash? Sixty-eight days of treatment for our son cost us in the low $40,000 range, while we spoke with a parent who sent their child to another program (in the same state) and the same 68 days cost them $75,000. I, Michelle, had a large lump sum due when my son arrived at the facility which covered the first 30 days of treatment as well as all the supplies he would need while out in the field. We would then receive a weekly bill until his discharge. In the months before sending our son away we had taken out a Home Equity Line of Credit to do some home remodeling, so we were able to dip into that line of credit to make the payments for his treatment. Another parent told us that they used their child's college fund. The dad originally was against the idea of using this money, voicing the argument of how will they pay for college? The mom's response was: "if we don't get her treatment there is a good chance she won't be alive to go to college." That child got the treatment she needed and is now healthy and enrolled in a local community college. Taking out an educational loan is another option. Just be cautious and make sure that the loan will cover the program you have chosen as these loans often have strict guidelines. If you have already established a 529 college fund you can pull money from that to help cover expenses. We do recommend speaking with your financial advisor prior to going these two routes. While this next option can be exceedingly difficult to do, it can also be very beneficial, and that is: Ask for financial assistance. Jenny was fortunate that Lucy's father's work had an emergency employee assistance program, and they were able to receive a grant from them. Other parents have gone to grandparents, friends, and family to ask for financial assistance. Donation Crowdfunding such as GoFundMe and reaching out to your local place of worship are other options. When calling programs make sure to ask if they offer any assistance/scholarships. Some programs will have a scholarship program or will work with you on the price. It is not widely advertised that this is an available option, but it is out there, you just need to ask. Several nonprofits will assist financially to help cover the expense of wilderness therapy. The first I'd recommend is a nonprofit based out of California called, Sky's the Limit (skysthelimitfund.org) which helps youth in crisis by providing information on wilderness therapy programs, coaching services to assist families with the transition home as well as offering grant money to those that need financial assistance. Saving Teens (savingteens.org) is a nonprofit that also helps families in need by providing education consultants either pro bono or at a greatly reduced rate, as well as assisting in finding scholarships and support before, during, and after placement. The Jason William Hunt Foundation (jwhf.org) is a nonprofit in Ohio that will provide financial aid to at-risk kids who attend a wilderness therapy program. The

LOA fund helps young adults (18-30) with the cost of wilderness therapy (Loafund.com). Charles N Miller scholarship will assist with tuition costs for a low-income teen from the Southeastern States (Charlesnmillerscholarship.com). The Parker Bounds Johnson Foundation will assist with those who are in the states of Oregon and Washington and need to attend a wilderness therapy program (pbjf.org). These programs offer more than just financial support, they also offer other resources and support. Lastly, wilderness therapy is considered a medical expense so you would be able to deduct the cost from your taxes. Parents have even deducted travel expenses that they occurred to get their child to the program. While you would still have to pay upfront, you would at least get some back at tax time.

Wilderness therapy is still considered an experimental treatment; therefore, most insurances will not cover the cost and the facilities will not even accept the insurance. Some families have been able to get their insurance to pay for the therapeutic cost that occurred while there, only after filing several appeals with the insurance company. After my son was discharged from wilderness therapy we sent the bills to the insurance company in hopes of some reimbursement and out of the $40,000+ we spent, we received around $150 back from insurance. Some organizations will assist families in the appeal processes with insurance companies. Both Jenny and I hired such a company, and they were able to file all the appeal paperwork on our behalf. Neither of us was successful in obtaining any additional reimbursement but at least we knew that we tried all avenues available to us. The good news though is that parents and mental health advocates are starting to fight back against the insurance companies, arguing that this is NOT experimental therapy, and it can be extremely beneficial for many kids. So, while it is a huge expense we felt it was worth it to get our children the help they needed.

The University of New Hampshire conducted a study regarding the effectiveness of wilderness therapy. In an article dated September 24, 2019 they share the results that show wilderness therapy is both more effective and more cost efficient than traditional therapy options. Link included in book citations.

EXCERPT FROM LETTER WRITTEN BY DREW TO THE INSURANCE COMPANY ON WHY WILDERNESS THERAPY WORKED FOR HIM:

"There is no accountability in traditional therapy, I could just tell the therapist that I will try harder next time or just lie about how I was doing. But in wilderness, I had constant accountability. The staff and other kids there would not let me get away with acting up. They always called me out and pushed me to confront my emotions head-on. In traditional therapy, there was no honesty and no trust but at ***** I felt that I could be honest with the people there because they were in the exact same situation that I was in, I also knew that in order to be in the group I was in I had to fit a very specific criteria so there was no way I could make myself any better or any worse emotionally. Another big reason that wilderness worked is that there was positive peer pressure. The other kids there would peer pressure me in my early days to get vulnerable and talk about my emotions which was an extremely odd thing to do. Some more reasons that ***** worked is because I realized that I had hit a real bottom and realized that my life running on my terms was not working and it ended with me living in the woods, so I knew that I had to ask for help from everyone and humble myself. They taught real-life skills at ***** that I am still applying to my life today. I do not remember a single thing that was said in therapy. At ***** I also learned how to effectively talk out my negative feelings with other people so that I don't build resentments over small things"

MYTHS & OTHERS CONCERNS

Jenny and I would like to start out by acknowledging that while we were extremely fortunate in finding a wonderful program that worked for our families, we are also aware that not all programs are the same. In researching Wilderness Therapy programs, you will find many negative stories and opinions. In the '70s, '80s, and 90's there were numerous horror stories regarding wilderness therapy programs including corporal punishment, withholding of food, and even death of some children. At that time, these programs were not regulated, which allowed for some of the mistreatment to happen. Due to new regulations, research, best practice, reviews, and groups on the internet as well as whistle blowers, these dangerous facilities have been closed down. Some wilderness programs even got together to form the Outdoor Behavioral Health Council, in an effort to find the best practice for safety at the facilities. Yet, we are aware that not all programs are perfect and that there are still occurrences of mistreatment at some programs, this is where diligent vetting of a program is important. A wilderness therapy staff member told us that while these stories are based on true history, it is in the past and not an indication of how the facilities are today.

The troubled teen industry has been flooding all media outlets in an attempt to get the message out regarding the dangers of wilderness therapy. Many of the stories shared happened years before all the changes in the industry. We recommend that if this is a concern for you, check out the All Kinds of Therapy web page (allkindsoftherapy.com) where you will find two blog post that specifically address changes in wilderness therapy over the years. The first is, "12 Ways Teen Treatment has Changed Since Paris Hilton Went to CEDU" from August 27, 2020 and the other is "9 Outdated Half-Truths About the Troubled Teen Industry" dated July 27, 2020

One big misconception is that Wilderness Therapy is also a military-style boot camp. Up through the 1990s, there was not such a defined line between the two, but as the times have changed so has the approach to therapy. In a boot camp if the child says "NO" they will be coerced into behaving or even receive a punishment if they refuse. In Wilderness Therapy, if a child says "NO" they will receive support and guidance as they help the child transition to "YES." Boot camp is more punitive while Wilderness is more supportive. Wilderness therapy believes in relationship modification. This is where the child is treated as you would want to be treated - think of "The Golden Rule" (treat others as you want to be treated). When people are treated with love and understanding the heart begins to change and healing will come naturally. It should also be noted that corporal punishment and withholding food are not allowed in these programs. Regarding corporal punishment, staff are not allowed to touch a child unless it is for a safety concern.

People also believe that only "bad" kids go to Wilderness Therapy. Many good kids struggle during their teen years with anxiety, drug abuse, anger, and many other emotional and psychological diagnosis. The goal of Wilderness Therapy is to get the child away from the environment that has been toxic to them and into an environment that is both supportive and encouraging. Kids thrive when they are around other kids who are sharing the same struggles they are. Since the program is a revolving system with kids being admitted and discharged there will always be teens there with more wilderness time under their belt. My son told me that he learned so much from these kids who were in the program ahead of him. They were able to help him navigate the program and encouraged him to start working on himself.

encourages growth + builds positive peer role models.

The weather is a concern that is often expressed. Either it will be too hot or too cold, too rainy or too windy. The staff is constantly monitoring the weather and if there are conditions that are not appropriate for the kids to be out in, they will bring them all back to base camp. The equipment my son received when he went into the woods/mountains in February was far superior to anything we have ever purchased. He stated that he stayed plenty warm even on the coldest nights. And let us be honest, a lot of these kids have never experienced a moment of discomfort in their lives, and sometimes discomfort is just what they need. One morning my son woke up in a puddle of water from rain the night before, and he thought it was great that he slept out in the rain. It was an "I can do it" moment. It is moments like these where kids learn that they are resilient, and their confidence grows. So, while he was uncomfortable, he was still 100% safe.

20

The majority of teens I know live on a diet of fast food, soda and sweets so when they get to the woods their diet will actually improve. Kids will complain about the food because they are getting healthier food than they ate prior. The variety was not particularly great in our teens' program, but they ate a healthy, balanced, high-calorie diet that took into account all the activities the kids were doing. With proper nutrition, the kids will feel better both physically and mentally, therefore giving them the energy they need to work on themselves. My son entered the program unhealthy and underweight, yet he left the program at a healthy weight, with muscle growth, and feeling physically great. While a friend he made in the program came in overweight he was able to shed his extra pounds and get to a healthy weight with the proper nutrition and exercise.

I have heard many parents say they are afraid that by sending their child away the child will become resentful of them or that they may even develop PTSD (especially those that were transported). While I am sure that this has happened and will continue to happen with some kids, we have found this to not be a common occurrence. At first, the child will of course be angry and resentful, but once the program starts to work they will often have a mind shift and realize that they are in the right place at the right time. When you get that letter home from your child saying "thank you for sending me here" you will realize that all you and your child have gone through was worth it.

One of my concerns in sending my child away was, who was going to be with him all day and night? I found out that they will be with young adults who are passionate about the outdoors and with helping others. The majority of them are college-educated and even have wilderness training in their background. Former wilderness therapy participants will often come back years later and join the staff. They feel that they received so much from their time in the wilds that they want to give back to others who are now struggling just like they had. Even though not all are not licensed counselors our children found the program alumni very insightful and a huge part of their growth. In these counselors, they found someone who understood them because they had once been in the same situation. A hiring manager at a wilderness therapy program told me that when she is hiring field staff some of the things she looks for in a candidate are the following: have a background in the back country, a therapy background, experience working with kids, been there/done that candidates, people that are able to do hard work without quitting, able to show compassion, able to model positivity for the kids, and the ability to control their egos and show humility. An interesting quality she looks for is a worker who can take and accept feedback from the kids. These kids are very vocal and not afraid to say what is on their minds, so the staff must be able to listen to and accept what the kids have to say, whether it is positive or negative. The guides are all a minimum of 21 years old, though they are usually more in their late 20's to early 30's due to increased maturity. All facilities will have different criteria as to their hiring practices so this would be a good question to ask when you are vetting programs.

min age of staff hired in programs

WHY WILDERNESS THERAPY?

We feel that there are many benefits to a wilderness program but the overall benefits we found was that it improved our kids' mental, emotional and behavioral health. It taught them coping strategies and skills and lastly it helped to improve family relations.

While at the program your teens are not going anywhere. They are safe, they are getting exercise as well as eating and sleeping properly. Being removed from everyday life and not having a place to hide, such as their room playing video games, is not an option, therefore, they are able to fully engage in the program and have no outside distractions. A combination of all of the above gives them many opportunities to work on themselves. Many teens enter the program with low self-esteem and confidence, but when they survive and even thrive in this environment it will be life-changing for them and boost their self-esteem and confidence. The benefits of being in nature have been found to be overwhelming. Being out in nature is known to decrease aggressive behavior, increase self-confidence and self-esteem as well as boost your mood, help to build social connections, decrease loneliness, and decrease anxiety and depression. One thing my child mentioned was that it helped him to stop the repetitive negative thoughts he always carried with him. An interesting read is a book by Richard Louv, "Last Child in the Woods: Saving our Children from Nature-Deficit Disorder." It talks about how children and teens are "nature deficient" and what a powerful tool nature can be in helping with mental health and development, and what can happen if that connection is lost.

I could share statistics and research with you that show the benefits of wilderness therapy and why it works, but instead, I am going to share thoughts from a woman who participated in a program as a teenager and went on to work for several programs in different capacities. In summary, she says: As humans, we are far removed from the natural world, removed from nature, tranquility, and quiet. We are designed to face struggles and discomfort in life, but in this current world we live in, we are removed from a lot of adversity that we should be dealing with. When we are able to face the struggles and discomfort, that is when we will learn resilience and grow. Kids need to immerse themselves in nature and take away distractions, such as social media and phones. They need to still their mind and learn how to develop connections with others. They will learn that what one person does, thinks, and feels will affect the group as a whole. They will learn gratitude and lose their sense of self-entitlement. They will learn to separate what is real and what is superficial and inconsequential. When out in nature and in a program that utilizes relational modification (where the child is treated as you would want to be treated) all the above changes just happen organically.

Part of the magic of Wilderness therapy is that the teens have the opportunity to gain knowledge and valuable skills through experiences that can be related to their life at home. All of this will aid in their recovery journey. As they hike, camp, and live in the Wilderness with a group, they discover what it means to be responsible for themselves physically, mentally, and emotionally as well as their impact on others.

The program is also designed for the teens to learn what it means and what it is like to be a part of a community and respect others. They are taught Expedition Behavior – which is the mindset necessary for them to make good decisions for themselves and their group. The teens are expected to pull their own weight (take care of self and gear and help carry group gear), be a productive member of the group (participate in all aspects of camp maintenance, support other members and give honest feedback to other), always work hard both physically and emotionally and lastly; to show leadership to the group. During the day to day routine your child will be learning both hard and soft skills. The hard skills they will learn are considered to be Wilderness Skills and they can be translated into life skills which are also known as soft skills. As they learn to master the hard skills, they will be practicing and become proficient in the soft skills. While practicing these skills they were also expected to write in their journals throughout the process. Below is a list of the hard skills they learned and what soft skills it represents.

HARD SKILLS	SOFT SKILLS
Striking Fires	Goal Setting
Marking Traps	Patience
Making natural cordage	Active Listening
Bow Drilling	Conflict Resolution
Hiking	Leadership
Plant Identification	Mindfulness
Map and Compass	Organization
Tent Setting	Communication
Academic Lessons	Time Management
Camping	Tolerance

In addition to the hard and soft skills, our program also had several phases the kids had to master. Each phase is considered to be completed once each of the objectives has been met. At that point, the teen can move to the next phase, but not before. The phases are designed to help them learn certain skills and provide the opportunity for them to take responsibility for themselves and learn the values that are important to them. The phases may have different names depending on the wilderness location you choose as well as the program your teen is in. However, each phase will build on the previous one and are explained below.

Phase 1:

In this phase, your teen will learn to think positively about themselves. They practice looking internally to better understand their feelings and beliefs.

Phase 2:

During this phase, the teen will learn hour to take accountability for their actions. They will be asked to practice positive leadership skills in order to help their group. They will be expected to function as a role model as well as learn how to address their group appropriately.

Phase 3:

With this phase, your teen will be expected to take ownership of their performance within the group as well as actively lead and teach within the group.

Phase 4:

This is the last phase. The teen will be expected to continue practicing what they have learned during each phase and then apply that knowledge to successfully prepare for their next step in their life as they transition out of wilderness.

Each phase has a checklist that has to be signed off on by a staff person before transitioning to the next phase. Your teen must be able to demonstrate their knowledge successfully and then petition for the next phase. They will lead a Petition Round where they will explain why they are ready to transition to the next phase and then request feedback from the group. They will then be expected to write about the feedback received from their peers and instructors in their journals.

As your teen begins to complete these phases, their therapist will be making transition plans for graduation and moving on to the next phase of your teen's life.

Parents will often struggle with what therapeutic option should be tried first. Wilderness therapy, therapeutic boarding school, residential treatment facilities, partial hospitalization programs, intensive outpatient programs – the list of options is endless. In speaking with other families, it seems like the most positive outcomes were when the kids started at Wilderness therapy. While in the wilderness the kids are engaged in therapy 24/7 with no outside distractions, it is a "hard reset" for the child. Once they have successfully completed their time in the wilderness program they will next transition to the next phase of recovery where there is more freedom and re-introductions to those outside distractions.

For additional information check out: SoundCloud.com – How Wilderness Therapy Works, Episode 111 as well as the article "How Wilderness Therapy Helps to Deal with Depression" by Monica Jenner.

GETTING TO THE WOODS

The next big question after you decide to send your teen to the woods, is" How will I get them there?" Most wilderness programs give the parent the option to either drop their teen off or have a transportation service bring them from your home to the site. To the kids, this process is known as "gooning." As soon as I, Jenny, heard that word, my immediate reaction was "What a horrible word!" and "What kind of parent has to do this?" Me, I was that parent. Upon registering your teen for the wilderness, you will work with the admissions team to determine their start date. Once that is established, you will then determine what transportation options are best for your situation.

Initially, I, Michelle, was advised by my teen's counselor to not tell him he was being sent away. But we could tell that he *might* be ready to get the help he needed. So, we sat down with him and asked him if he was willing to do whatever was needed to get his life straightened out and to get the help we could tell he so needed. Since he said he was willing to do whatever it took, we thought it would bring him relief to explain that we found a place in the woods where he could stay for a while to work on himself and heal emotionally. Thankfully, he had always enjoyed being outside hunting and fishing, so this sounded good to him. We did not give him many details regarding the program as we were afraid that if we told him too much, he would change his mind and refuse to go. He told us later that he thought he would be able to skate, play basketball, and lounge around in front of the TV.

We were told to be at the facility at a specific date and time and the drop-off was a brief process of checking in and a quick goodbye. As we were heading to the facility the morning of drop-off, he was in the back seat texting with friends telling them that he was NOT going to give up his phone and that if he did not like it, he was going to run away. We just let him continue with his texting because we did not want to start trouble when we were so close to getting him where he needed to be. When we arrived at the facility, we went straight into the office where the administration staff was waiting for us. They called the field staff to let them know that we were there so they could head over to get him. We were told to say our goodbyes and they stepped away to give us privacy. After the final hug and kiss, the field staff took him out of the building to start his intake process. All this occurred in less than 15 minutes. The administrator then took my husband and me into another room so we could talk and ask any questions. The facility nurse came in to meet us so we could review his medications and ask her questions as well. We were then given a very quick and short tour of the facility. We were able to see the food pantry and check out all the equipment that was going to be issued to him. Parents and kids were kept separate, so we were not able to see much, as they did not want us to accidentally meet up again. I cannot even begin to explain how I felt that day. It was a cold, dreary, and rainy day when we dropped him off which I found so fitting. As we were sitting in the office talking with staff I could hear a kid outside crying, and I was convinced it was my son. I wanted to run out of the room and hug that child, whether he was my child or not. Every person I talked to for the next week I would ask them "was that my child crying?" Everyone said no, but until my son came home and told me that it was not him, all I could think of was him sitting right outside that window and crying. I tried to put off leaving for as long as possible so I could at least be in the same vicinity as my child, even if I could not see him. Finally, I just had to turn and walk away, praying that we had made the correct decision for our son and our family. Since our child knew that he was going to treatment once he got to the facility he was able to immediately get to work on himself and did not have to deal with the emotions of being sent away unexpectedly. With kids who are transported, they will often need an extra few weeks in the program as they need time to adjust to the fact that they are in treatment and had no idea it was going to happen. A wilderness therapy staff member told me that they believe if at all possible it is best to let your child know up front that they are going to be going away for treatment. Yet, we all know that this is not always possible. If a transport company is needed then they recommend that the parents be present during the process and that they tell the child what is going on.

If you will need a transport company, be sure to ask the following questions:

**How long has the company been in business?

**Do they have insurance? Business, Auto, and Workers Comp.

**How do you hire? Do you do background checks?

**What sort of training do you provide?

**Do you have any official relationships with the facilities?

**What is your policy on restraints?

If you choose to have your teen transported the site will work with you on either recommendation of companies that do this or explain their own transport process. Some programs will do the transport themselves. I encourage you to consider both options and really think about what will be best for you, your teen, and all that may be involved. Transportation or intervention services can be recommended by the wilderness program of your choice. These companies will focus on providing safe and confidential transportation and transition to the programs and they specialize in working with teens. The staff who work for these services are highly trained and well versed in how to anticipate every move of your teen. I, Jenny, was given a full bio of the people that would be with my teen and was allowed to interview them. One of the people that transported my teen was a retired Army Ranger. When I asked him why he did this job, he said, "Every kid deserves a second chance to get the help they need, and I like being a part of something good." The staff are trained to look for any attempts to run or escape as well as how to deal with severe anger and violent reactions; and have a plan for how to respond. Two agents, known as interventionists, pick your teen up, catching them by surprise, and take them to the program. Their goals are to ensure safety during the transport, communicate with the parent, and educate and support the teen emotionally as they transition from home to being in a treatment program.

When the decision was made to send my daughter to the woods, I knew beyond a shadow of a doubt she would not go willingly. Her addiction was so strong, she lied constantly about the addiction, and had no desire to quit nor ask for help. I was also scared that if I could actually get her into the car to drive to the location, she might do something crazy like try to jump out, become violent towards me or run away from home forever. Once I learned about this option, I had no doubt, that transport was my only choice. It was also an excessively big and bold first step to show her how serious I was about this decision and that she was going to treatment, no matter what.

The company I chose was wonderful, and they held my hand the entire time. They understood and allowed space for all of my tears and questions while calming my many fears. They offered training, how-to videos, and the opportunity to talk to other parents that used their services in the past. Depending on the program you select, and its proximity to your home, they offer both driving and flying options. I can honestly say they made one of the hardest days of my life somewhat tolerable. The training and support that they provided for me prepared me for the day that she left home to start her therapy; and although I was a nervous wreck, I was well prepared mentally and physically. Once I made the decision, a phone call was set for me to help them plan out all of the coordination of her transportation. The company walked me through every single step, and it was obvious nothing was overlooked. Because my teen had no idea what was being planned, they suggested I have our meeting in a secluded location so there was no chance my daughter could overhear anything. They spent a lot of time with me preparing me for what the process would look like and what my role would be. They asked extremely detailed questions about the layout of my house, where her room was located, where all the doors were located, where her phone would be at the time of their arrival, and what I expected her reaction could be. The three questions that still play in my head that were mind-blowing for me were, "What are the escape routes in your house in case she decides to run? What does she have in her room that she could use as a weapon? Will she be violent with us? "Escape routes? Weapons? Are you kidding me??" I had never thought of such things. There are so many things in this journey that blindside you at times and make it hard to even breathe. Thinking of my home as a place with an escape route and her potential use of weapons was definitely one of those times. However, it did confirm to me that I was doing the right thing.

The transport company also helped plan out what I would say to my daughter when they got to my house, which was a huge help. I still remember the look in her eyes when I told her she was being sent away. It was so painful, but I knew I had finally gotten her attention and she knew I would not tolerate her behaviors and choices anymore. The transport company's diligence was excellent. We went over everything, including where I should park my car in the driveway so they could have their vehicle as close as possible to the front door, what my daughter would be sleeping in so she was appropriately dressed in front of strangers, how they would manage things if she got violent, and the communication plan once she was taken out of my home. They even recommended that my younger teen stay with a friend that night so he was not a part of whatever may happen. I was assured they would communicate via text throughout the transportation process, and they did just that. All details had been covered, including an extra outfit laid out for her to wear, along with shoes and a bag for her destination. She was not allowed to shower or get ready. They picked her up "as is" and assured me that most teens did not get violent. They would take diligent care of her.

They arrived at my home between 5:30 and 6 am on the pre-arranged day. I had taken my daughter's phone about 30 minutes before their arrival, and she was sound asleep. The element of surprise was critical for us, as she had to be caught off guard. There was a male and a female, and they were both exceedingly kind and professional. I was a teary mess and did not sleep at all the night before. I had practiced what to say over and over, but I was still very shaky and nervous. We went over the details once more on my front porch so she could not hear anything, and then set things into motion. I knew there was no going back, and I knew, beyond any doubt, that this was the only option I had to save my daughter's life.

They offered me some encouraging words, and they even asked me about her favorite breakfast place so they could feed her along the way (Chick-fil-a). I was fortunate that there was a wilderness treatment center less than three hours from where we lived so I did not have to wait that long to hear how things went.

I entered her room as they stood outside her door, and I will never forget the words I said at that moment.

Me - Honey, I need you to wake up, I have something important to tell you.

Her - what the f*&$, mom, I'm sleeping?

Me – I need you to listen carefully to what I am about to tell you. I have made the decision to get you the help you desperately need, and there are people here to take you to the place where this will happen.

Her - What? (shocked, confused, and still half asleep)

Me - I am sending you away to get help, and these people (called them by name and they entered the room) will take you there. You are in good, safe hands.

Her - (screaming and begging) No Mom, no! I'll stop using and I'll be better, please don't!"

Me - I love you too much not to do this. I believe in you and know you will be successful.

I tried to hug her, and she pulled away, glared at me with one of the most horrible looks she had ever given me, and told me she hated me. I then left my house as they advised. I was fighting tears, trying not to cry and as soon as I got to my car, I did not fight them and collapsed in tears.

The staff members communicated everything along the way via text. This was purposeful as they did not want to have any conversation she could hear. They let me know when they had gotten her to the car and were leaving town. They gave me updates on her mood and any questions she asked. They offered to feed her breakfast, which she refused. She asked if she could stop for the restroom, which they did allow, but she was walked in with the female staff person, and they stayed right outside the stall door as their eyes were always on her. The female staff person sat in the back seat with her so that she was always within arm's reach. I was told that statistically, most kids become compliant quickly and do not display violence once the parent is no longer around. I was glad to hear that she did not become violent, and from the time I entered her room to the time they pulled out of my driveway, less than 30 minutes had passed.

Upon her arrival at the program site, they texted me to let me know they had arrived safely, with a promise to call once the handoff had been made. True to their word, this is exactly what happened. At that time, they answered every question I had, gave me a detailed verbal report of the interaction, her demeanor throughout the trip, and how she seemed at the time of drop-off. The program site also called to let me know she was in their custody. As I mentioned in the beginning, they made one of the worst days of my life as bearable as possible. I am deeply grateful for this option and if I had to do it all over again, I have no doubt I would handle it in the exact same way.

I have spoken with other parents who shared a similar experience with the companies they went with. These companies understand how hard this is for the families they are helping and are very empathetic while maintaining professionalism the entire time. Even though these people were strangers, I knew she was safer with them, much more than with her drug-addicted friends.

Regardless of how you decide to transport your teen to the wilderness program, it will be an emotional day. There is no easy path to get there. But I passionately believe that from the moment she was taken from my house, I was able to start on the path to my healing and becoming a better parent for her as well as learn how to support her sobriety.

⑥ what was the daughter using?

WHAT IS MY ROLE NOW?

Once your teen is safely in the woods the first thing you need to do is take a deep breath and relax. There is a good chance that once you are able to take that deep breath and relax for a bit, you will feel great peace. That peace is a wonderful thing but along with that peace there is often the feeling of "I'm glad my teen is not here – I'm a horrible parent." Please know that you are not the only parent who has felt this way and that there is nothing wrong with this feeling. You have been living a life of turmoil and anxiety and it is only natural that once that stressor (your teen) is temporality removed from the situation, you will feel better. Some parents will feel terrible or guilty for deciding to seek this particular avenue of treatment. Those of you need to know that you are an incredibly strong parent, you are a parent who is willing to do whatever it takes to get your child the help that they need, you need to be proud of yourself. Regardless of how you are feeling, it does not mean that you get to sit home and do nothing while your teen is out of the house. This is the time for you to start working on yourself, to heal old wounds, and re-center yourself.

First, I would recommend taking some time for just you. Go on a date night, get a pedicure or play a round of golf. Do something just for you – something that YOU enjoy. While you are out doing this fun activity focus your conversation on something other than your teen. This is your time. Throughout the time your teen is away it is important to continue to make time for yourself.

Reading is going to be a new pastime for you. Find books that explain wilderness therapy, addiction, parenting skills, etc. The important thing here is to consume as much information as you can to help for when your teen comes home. The first book I read was "The Parallel Process" by Krissy Pozatek. This book explains in more detail what happens in the woods and how you, the parent, can start the process of learning and healing. "The Parental Toolbox – for Parents & Clinicians" by Dayna Guido and Jim Guido is another book that helped us during this journey. Podcasts are another great tool. There are podcasts on every topic you could ever think of. Use them! Learn from them. The wonderful thing about the books and podcasts is that you will find out you are not alone. Up until now, you have more than likely felt all alone and like there is no one else out there who understands what you have been going through. Just knowing that there are others out there who do understand and who have been in your situation is such a great feeling.

The facility that your teen is at will also offer family counseling sessions. Programs will differ as to who is invited to be in these family therapy sessions. In the program we choose these sessions were just me, my husband, and the counselor. My other son was invited to join as well if he wanted. Some programs will allow the teen in the program to join in these sessions. Although these will be over the phone, they are greatly beneficial. During these sessions, we were able to discuss what led up to us sending our teen away and how things will be different once he comes home. We also had the counselor teach us the therapeutic skills that our son was learning. This way we would all be on the same page regarding terminology and skills when he came home.

Weekly conversations with your teen's therapist will also occur. Fridays at 11 am was the highlight of my week because I was able to talk to someone who had seen and been with my son. During these conversations, a lot of information is shared. We would get an update as to my son's progression through the program and any issues he was working through that week. I was able to ask questions as to how he was doing as well as pass on information that I felt would be beneficial to the counselor regarding providing the best therapy possible. These sessions are also when discharge planning takes place. My husband and I definitely felt that the entire process of communication with the facility was an inclusive team approach.

Having a teen in Wilderness therapy is not just a "kid" issue, it's a "family" issue, therefore, the whole family needs intervention. Many of these kids feel that they alone are working on their issues, but to hear that you, the parent, is also working on stuff will lift them up. Kids will often struggle both during their time away and once home if the parents do not put in the work to improve themselves. It is recommended that in each of your letters you tell your teen what you are reading or listening to. Share with them that you are also seeking your own therapy.

If you can find a local support group for parents, utilize it. Nothing helps more than talking with other parents who "get it" and utterly understand the life you have been living. For several years I had been suffering in silence. Thinking that there was no one out there who could ever understand the pain I have been feeling. Nobody who I could talk to that would not judge me or my child. Nobody that I could just relax and be honest with. Over a year after my son has returned from Wilderness therapy some of my dearest truest friends are those that I met in a parent support group that I attended. If your teen is struggling with addiction, I highly recommend finding a local PAL meeting (Parents of Addicted Loved Ones). Meetings.palgroup.org/meeting or call 480.300.4712. Facebook has numerous private groups for parents struggling with their teen whether it be addiction, mental illness, or behavioral issues. There are also groups that are dedicated to wilderness therapy, therapeutic boarding schools, and residential living facilities. If there are no support groups near you there is a website called, "Other Parents like Me" (Oplm.com). The paid membership to this site includes online support meetings, speakers, and resources from books to podcasts. During one of our first counseling sessions with the staff therapist, we asked about additional resources and he was able to get us the information for an organization located near where we lived that could provide support for our children after discharge. Thankfully, they also had a parent support group that was beneficial to our family.

Family therapy is also a great tool. The parents' and siblings' feelings, emotions, and issues will also need to be processed. Take this opportunity when things are calmer at home to focus on yourself and healing the family.

EXCERPT FROM LETTER HOME

**I also appreciate you guys seeking help because you're right, although I do need help, it's not just me

EXCERPTS FROM PARENT LETTERS:

**We found a new therapist that we (your Dad & I) are going to see together Monday morning"

**We are still going to the support group for parents. Everyone is very easy to relate to and there is no judgment."

A DAY IN THE WOODS

When our teens arrived at the facility, the first thing that happened was the intake process. During this time, a counselor completed a mental health screening to evaluate what their needs may be. They were bodily checked for any contraband such as weapons or drugs. It was especially hard when their phones were taken from them. While this is difficult for the teen, it is one of the greatest gifts we can give our kids. Being able to disconnect from the world is an opportunity for them to reconnect with themselves. In the program where our kids went, they also received new clothes. All the kids were issued matching pants, t-shirts, sweatshirts, outerwear, and even new hiking boots. In the colder months, they are given insulated clothing. The only item allowed from home was fourteen pairs of underwear. Thongs for girls were not allowed as they are considered a safety risk. With everyone having the same clothes, there were no issues surrounding who has nicer stuff, no threat of kids stealing from each other, and the reassurance that each teen would be properly outfitted for whatever kind of weather issues may happen.

online see as dehumanizing. Here, keeps perspective in safety and that status doesn't make you, you.

Kids were then issued their backpacks, which became their responsibility for the duration of their stay. The packs included all their clothing, food, and sleeping items. The sleeping bags that they were given were rated sub-zero, so they were plenty warm for the colder nights. Spread throughout all of the kids' packs were cooking gear, tools, and the portable toilet. Using the bathroom in the woods took some getting used to. The bathroom was kept behind a tarp so the kids would have privacy. It consisted of a bucket with a bag in it. The kids would carry the bucket, but the counselors would carry the bags. If a girl was menstruating, she would have to use pads, which were disposed of in the bags as well. Since the bathroom was behind a tarp, the kids would need to make noise while using it so the counselors would know they were not trying to run away. In fact, whenever a teen was out of sight from the counselors, they would have to make noise such as repeating their name over and over, singing a song, or banging sticks together. This noise requirement was also for medical safety as well as flight risk prevention. If a child was to stop making noise the counselor would be alerted to go check on the child to make sure nothing had happened to them such as passing out or running away. After changing into their new clothes and getting their pack set up, they got to meet their assigned peer group. Group size varied as kids entered and exited the program. My son's program had anywhere from 2-6 kids at one time, while a friend in another group had 6-14.

So, what does a typical day look like? This is how it was explained to me by two boys who went through a wilderness program. One went due to anger issues and the other due to drug abuse. Both of them told similar stories.

They woke up around 8 am (or so they thought). They had no watches or phones, so this was just a guess on their part. Not knowing the time was beneficial to them as they could stay in the present and not think back on what they would be doing if they were not in the woods. As my son told me, "if I knew it was 2:30 then I'd have thought of getting out of school and what my afternoon plans would be, and I wouldn't have been focusing on what I was doing right then". Upon waking they would cook their breakfast with a pot heated by propane. Breakfast consisted of oatmeal or grits and spices/flavoring. Each teen was issued a bowl, a cup, and a spoon that they were responsible to keep track of and keep clean. Once everyone finished eating their initial serving of food, the pot was passed around again so the kids could get seconds. During this time, they had "morning circle" where each teen would rate their sleep from the night before and do some FAB-C's. A FAB-C (Feelings/About/Belief-Choice) is a way to rate your feelings and attitudes. For example, I FEEL angry / ABOUT being here / my BELIEF is I do not want to be here / my CHOICE is that I will accept being here. FAB-Cs were used frequently throughout the day. By using an "I feel" statement your child is taking responsibility for their feelings, and not laying blame on others. I was told by my son that when he first entered the program he was not able to identify his feelings, let alone express them. By using this model, he learned how to identify, understand and even express how he was feeling. This is also a great tool for parents to learn as it will help with communication when your teen comes home.

After clean-up from camp breakfast, they reviewed the list of upcoming daily activities, and the staff would give out personal goals for each teen to work on. Activities may be anything from a reminder to drink at least three bottles of water to their journaling goals. In our teen's program, they had a search and rescue journal that they had to work on daily. The journal included learning both soft and hard skills. A soft skill could be working on their communication while a hard skill would be bow drilling. An example journal topic might be: "Reflect on the stages of change; what stage do you see yourself in?" Or "Write a one page journal entry on: When was a time you used poor verbal communication and how could you have communicated more effectively?" After this review, they packed their backpacks and started hiking. They never knew for sure how far they had hiked each day, but they felt like it was several miles. They would hike for 5 days and then have 2 days where they would make a more permanent camp. During this 2-day layover, they would get their food stores restocked and the licensed therapist would come out to the field camp. As our teens progressed through the program, they were given more leadership roles which resulted in getting additional information from the staff, such as where they would be stopping for the night, or even be given the opportunity to lead the hike.

When it was time for lunch, they stopped hiking to make camp. Lunch consisted of pepperoni sticks, tuna, granola, cheese sticks, nuts, and dried fruits. Mac & Cheese day was always a big treat. On holidays and birthdays, the kids would get a special treat brought out to the campsite such as brownies. The kids in leadership roles did the cooking and they came up with some great combinations of food and flavoring.

EXCERPT FROM LETTER HOME

**I'm terrible at rationing, I'm probably going to advocate for more food because I'm always hungry, and ya I'm eating the cheese sticks.

**the food is decent depending on who makes it

The kids were responsible for all the camp set up and take down. They were taught LNT, which stands for "Leave No Trace." This is such a great tool for our kids to learn and it is something that transfers over to the world they will live in after discharge from the program. It teaches them to be considerate, think of the environment, and ultimately think of something other than themselves. After lunch, the kids would spend time working in their journals, writing letters home, or just relaxing around the campsite. The counselors sometimes led the kids in fun made-up games or just played cards. This time was also used to get the kids together for a group therapy session. The facility therapist would come out to the field once a week for individual therapy with each teen. During this time, our teen and their therapist would spend one on one time together talking about tools to deal with the issues with which they were struggling. Some programs also have a drug/alcohol therapist who will go into the field to meet with the teen. Therapy dogs are also a great benefit and are often found around the campsites. Working with dogs will often bring out the softer side of kids and help them show more vulnerability, they are more likely to let their guard down. The dogs will show unconditional love and loyalty to your child which helps them learn about safe relationships and what that looks like. Once they have a safe relationship with their dog, they begin to transfer those feelings over to humans. Canine therapy has been shown to increase coping skills, decrease anxiety, help the kids to become better communicators, and improve their social skills. Equine therapy has also proven to be beneficial for kids who are struggling. In these cases, the kids are assigned a horse that they are responsible for taking care of. By taking care of their own horse the teen and horse will develop a bond and they will begin to unselfishly care for the horse. Self-confidence will grow in the teen as they learn to care for and handle such a large animal. Horses are very perceptive to human emotions and even human facial expressions. This fact alone helps the teen learn about non-verbal communication. The teens will increase their self-awareness as they work with the horses, and this allows them to think about things in a new way. As the teen begins to connect with their horse they are also learning how to connect with people. Trust between horse and teen will cross over to trust between the teen and others.

Back at camp, once dinner came around, they cooked rice, beans, and lentils as their main dinner staple. A favorite dinner recipe of my sons was fried rice with vegetables seasoned with soy sauce, brown sugar, garlic powder, chili pepper, salt, and pepper. But before they would eat, they took time for PRT (personal reflection time), which is when they would sit quietly and reflect on their day. After dinner and cleaning up, they sat around a fire and had TC (truth circle). During this time, each kid did a nightly inventory where they got honest about questions such as: Were we resentful or selfish today, dishonest, afraid? Do we owe anyone an apology? Is there anything that needs to be addressed with another? Were we kind and loving? What could we have done better? Were we selfishly thinking of ourselves most of the day or thinking of how we could be of service to others? (Source: Alcoholics Anonymous Big Book, page 86.) Each teen also did a safety check where they rate how they were feeling on a 1-10 scale.

To get the conversation going an "open round" would sometimes be called. This is where someone calls out a question and each person around the circle responds to the question/comment. An example might be as simple as "what's your favorite food" to more in-depth questions, such as "what is holding you back from being vulnerable?" A serious round is where the teens answer the following questions: "Any thoughts of homicide, suicide, harm to self, harm to other, craving substances, self-deprecation, or grievances?" This is a great activity for all the kids but especially for those who are newer to the program. It is the beginning step of the teens learning to be vulnerable but with only having to say a simple "yes" or "no" answer. Teens would also share the highlight of their day and the low light of their day. During these circle times, the kids were given the opportunity to open up about any struggles they were going through. They could receive feedback from the other kids as well as from the counselors. The kids learned how to really listen and support others.

EXCERPT FROM LETTER HOME

***then we do TC, which is one of my favorite parts of the day*

In a true wilderness program, the kids are not sleeping in comfortable bunks in an air-conditioned or heated building. They are outside under the stars, sleeping under tarps or tents. This may sound harsh, but being out in nature, looking at the stars (and not social media) is very therapeutic for kids. One thing I still hear about is the wonderful scenery my teen saw and experienced. He was able to watch sunrises and sunsets over the mountains — something that he had never slowed down long enough to do at home.

EXCERPT FROM LETTER HOME:

***and my favorite thing I have seen was when I was camping in a valley, and it snowed the night before, so everything was white, and we all stood and watched the sun come up over the mountain and it shined on the snow, and it was beautiful*

Some questions I really struggled with were, "How does building a fire help my teen learn to control his anger? Shouldn't he be getting therapy every day?" Well, I learned that building a fire was his therapy. Learning to use a bow drill was his therapy. Building a fire with only flint and steel can be very frustrating and take days to learn, causing their anger and frustration to show its self. While dealing with frustration over the fire, they are learning skills to deal with the frustrations that they encounter in life. As the teen progresses through the program, they move up in levels, and each level presents a new more challenging skill they need to learn. Once they master a level, they have a profound sense of accomplishment and the drive to want to master the next level. That feeling of accomplishment in the woods will then be tied back to accomplishment or goals in the "real" world.

When groups of kids are together, conflict will naturally arise at some point. When this happens, the counselors who are with the kids 24/7 are able to address the issues immediately by having a conflict circle. They will help the conflicted kids figure out what the issue was, what potential triggers were, and how to resolve the issue calmly and peacefully. This is a time to focus on what you are feeling and ways to deal with these feelings.

There are times when a teen will not cooperate—they might go on a "hike strike." Meaning they refuse to get up and hike. When this happens, the counselors will spend time with the teen and try to find the underlying cause of why they do not want to hike. The other kids will often intervene and try to motivate the teen to get up and going. When my son first got to the facility, he refused to go out on the hike thinking that we would be coming back to get him once we realized what the program was like. The other kids in his group talked to him and convinced him that it was not so bad and to give it a try. Positive peer pressure can be a great tool if used in the right situations.

Accountability is also a huge factor in helping these kids out. Most kids, especially boys, do not talk about their feelings, but when all these feelings are bottled up, they often manifest in angry outbursts or drug use. In the woods, the kids are taught to be vulnerable and talk about everything.

It appears like a lot of the programs purposely have prolonged quiet time. One program had a 2-day quiet time when the teen first arrived. The reasoning was it gave the teen time to reflect on what had transpired in the past to get them to the point of being sent away, as well as time to think about what they wanted in life. In our children's program, the kids did 3 days separated from the group, only after they had been in the program for a few weeks. They would remain in sight of the main group but isolated — once again giving the teen a chance to reflect on where they have been, what they have learned up to that point, and where they want to go.

EXCERPT FROM LETTER HOME

**it was 3 days and 2 nights alone and I did a lot of journal work, prayed, and meditated a lot

In talking with several graduates of wilderness therapy I asked them "What did you learn and what skills are you still using today." The answers were pretty much the same regardless of the program they went to. The most common answers were:

**They are more grateful for their lives and the lives provided for them.

**They learned coping skills and how to accept their situation.

**They learned how to get vulnerable and talk about their feelings.

**They learned how to deal with anger and deal with conflict.

**They learned how to mediate.

**They learned basic social skills and how to communicate with others.

**They learned many outdoor skills such as: fire starting, bow drilling, trap making, tree and leaf identification.

FROM F-YOU TO THANK YOU

In the program, we choose the only form of communication between parent and teen was through letter writing. Some programs allow phone calls, either on a scheduled basis or an earned basis. Most programs require the same kind of letters which we will discuss and share parts. The first letter is from the teen to the parent: This letter is usually written shortly after the teen arrives at the facility. We were told to expect one or more of the following types:

THE "YOU SUCK" LETTER: In this letter, the teen is cursing out their parents, telling them how much they hate them and that everything is their fault.

EXCERPT FROM LETTER HOME:

**Why the f$#k did you send me here? I do not want to be sober.

**I do not understand why you took me out of school to send me here because I've been doing the same shit for a long time. This is crazy!

**I am still deciding if I want a relationship with you.

THE "I'M SO SORRY" LETTER: In this letter, your teen claims to finally understand that they have been misbehaving and that they will do whatever you want and will walk the straight and narrow.

EXCERPTS FROM LETTERS HOME:

**I know that if I ask you to pull me out, you're going to want other options to "fix" me. My first suggestion would be antidepressants

**Another option we could pursue is one on one session with my therapist where I actually tell the truth

THE "I DON'T BELONG HERE" LETTER: In this letter where your teen claims that all the other kids there are bad and so much worse than they are - and that they just do not fit in with them.

EXCERPT FROM LETTER HOME:

**This place is not meant for me; I know I used to do drugs, but I've been sober ever since I promised you I would stop. This place is not meant for me because although I am depressed and get anxious, I feel as though coming here was the most extreme option we could've pursued. This place is not for people like me

While receiving any one of these letters hurts, this is typical of teens in the program. The facility can pretty much guarantee that you will receive one of these or a combination of them.

The Impact letter is the first letter that the parent(s) will write to the teen. In this letter, the parent tells the teen how their actions and behaviors have affected the family. This is a chance for you, the parent, to finally have a voice and a platform where you are guaranteed that your teen will listen. This letter is a starting point for the therapist to begin working with your teen. Some programs will have the first letter from the parents be a Seeds of Greatness letter. In this letter, the parents talk about all of their child's goodness. This is a chance to build the child up with positivity and not to dwell on the recent conflicts and issues that have been going on.

EXCERPTS FROM IMPACT LETTERS

***We have been tiptoeing around you for fear of you losing your temper again – we have been held hostage to your moods for too long. Let us not forget you have been suspended from school four times this year alone*

***Or telling us you were going to see (a friend) then going to see (someone else) or breaking into construction sites to get high. Or trying to buy acid from (co-worker) at work*

***You are there so that you can learn what we already know. You are there to learn that you are strong, intelligent, and capable of incredible things.*

***First, we want you to remember we love you more than life itself. It may be hard to understand right now, but we wholeheartedly believe we have made the right decision for you to work on making healthier and much more positive decisions moving forward.*

***We think you need this so much because you are worth it.*

You may find this hard to believe, but this is by far the hardest thing we have ever done.

**We hope you will go through this program with a good attitude, let down your guard, know you are safe and in the company of people who are all working to get to a better place.

One of the most significant letters that a parent receives is the Letter of Accountability. Along with the first letter we received from our teen, this was the other letter that was hard to receive. This letter is usually written by your teen after they have been in the program for a few weeks and depending on how far along they are in the therapeutic process. In this letter, your teen will take responsibility for their actions, and they will tell you everything that they have done. You may not have known your teen was stealing from you, sneaking out of the house, or taking certain drugs - but after this letter, you will know all that they have done.

EXCERPT FROM LETTER HOME

**First, I would like to take accountability for my constant lying about everything from what homework I have, to where I was going, to lying about being sober. Whenever I was lying, I was doing it because I believed that what I wanted was best

**I would like to take accountability for not taking my medication and either selling it at school or snorting it in class. The possible consequences of this are potential addiction and getting caught selling/using

EXCERPT FROM PARENT RESPONSE TO THE ACCOUNTABILITY LETTER

**I want to thank you for the accountability letter you sent. I am sure that it was not easy to write but I want you to know that I appreciate the honesty. Taking responsibility for your actions is a great step in healing as well as a show of maturity. I am not going to go over each thing in the letter, but I just want you to know that all is forgiven. I love you and am looking forward to the future – not into the past*

**I have forgiven you for everything*

Last of all, while our teen was in the wilderness, we received and sent weekly letters, which was the only form of communication they allowed at the program. Typical information included what they have been doing, about the other kids in the group, and the progress they have been making in the program. When we were lucky, we even got answers to some of the questions we asked in our letters. It is important in your letters to tell your teen how proud you are of all that they are doing – do this in every single letter you send. I think letting them know that they are forgiven for all past transgressions is also very healing for your teen. The past is the past and it is time to look toward the future. This is so important for these kids to hear. Talk to them about what is going on in the family and just day-to-day information. And ask questions!

Depending on the circumstances, siblings and grandparents may be allowed to attach a letter to the parents' letter, and the teen is allowed to write back to them as well. We even had our two dogs "write" a letter to my son. He loved it and wrote back to them. Letters between your teen and friends are usually not allowed. We spoke with my son's therapist and told him that a friend wanted to send a letter. The friend was allowed to write one letter which the counselor would read and approve before passing it on to my son. The counselor said that it would probably be just a one-letter deal, but the letter from the friend was so encouraging and supportive that an exception was made. That friend actually wrote to my son weekly until he came home. We were told that this is extremely rare to happen, but it does not hurt to ask. We were allowed to attach a few photos to each letter. Pictures of the family (ones that also include the teen who is at wilderness), pets, and landscapes are cherished. Your teen may even ask for something specific. When my daughter asked for a picture of her cat, I knew things were headed in a good direction.

Pictures of friends, screenshots of social media, and drugs/alcohol are not allowed. I was told by several boys that they would look at the pictures all the time, especially before bed, when they would reflect on their family and how much they missed them. They would share their photos with the other kids, so I made it a point to send some pictures that would spark conversation. For example, I sent a picture of my son's broken arm so he could share that "fun" story. The facility also sent us several pictures each week of our teens. Those pictures were so exciting to get, we were able to see our teens and know that they were doing OK. Nothing would make me happier than getting a picture and seeing a huge smile on my son's face!

EXCERPTS FROM LETTERS HOME:

In the beginning of my stay at **** I felt resentful towards you guys for sending me here, but I've taken a step back and looked at the situation from your perspective and now all I can do is thank you for sending me to this shit hole

grateful feelings are still here

**I am learning how to identify my anger before it shows itself and I'm learning how to cope with it

**I would also like to thank you for not giving up on me even though I was very deserving of it

**My group is awesome. I never use that word but the people I am around are incredible

**Yes, I am glad to be here. Happier than I have ever been. I am so grateful to have been sent here and pulled out of the hole I was in. I am grateful to have been removed from the life I was living

**I need you to know that my addiction is not your fault. There was nothing you could have don

EXCERPTS FROM PARENT LETTERS:

***We are so proud of you and how well you are adapting. You jumped right in and started working, which is so impressive and makes us happy and proud. This is a great opportunity to learn about yourself – what makes you, you. And YOU are fantastic! Take advantage of all that is offered, and you will grow and soar*

***So, at some point, you will be coming home, and we need to talk about some stuff before that happens. I will be honest in saying that while I cannot wait for you to come home, I'm also nervous*

***Life is trudging along as usual. I work, clean, eat and sleep! I'm working on a new painting of a seaside with cliffs, houses and some boats. Dogs are doing good. They say "woof, woof, bow-wow, woof, bark, woof, bark bark!*

GRADUATION FROM THE WILDERNESS

When the staff determined that your teen is ready to leave the woods and take their next steps, the graduation process began. For us, Jenny and Lucy, our program graduation was a three-day experience to prepare both the teen and parents for their reunion, leaving the woods, and embarking on the next step in their journey. The final part of graduation is the actual graduation ceremony. It is a time of both excitement and apprehension.

There is much work that takes place to prepare both the teen and the parent for this transition and process. For us, there were weekly emails as well as conversations between parent and therapist and between therapist and teen to determine what happens next. Home contracts are determined, other treatment options are discussed, and final decisions are made about what happens at both the literal and figurative end of the trail. Some parents choose to hire an Education Consultant to be a part of these conversations. An educational consultant will work with you, your teen, and your teen's treatment team to assist with determining the best options for your teen. This includes programs, schools, and therapy available where you live, or residential treatment centers and other in-patient programs that can best meet your teen's short and long-term needs if coming home is not the best choice for your teen.

Once the graduation date has been determined, as excited as you may feel to see your teen, this can also be a very tough and emotional time as both the parent and teen will be dealing with the unknown of what is to come. While you will know when your child is coming home, they will not find out until the day you arrive. This is so the kids will not get distracted with their pending discharge and will continue to work on themselves. They usually have an idea that discharge is coming up due to their involvement in working on the post wilderness discharge planning that they participate in, they just will not know when it is actually going to happen. Most wilderness therapy graduation programs have an overnight component in which the parent spends the night in the woods with the teen to see what they have both achieved and experienced during their time in the woods.

For my daughter, graduation was a three-day process. It began with her joining others that were graduating at that same time to form the final graduating group. Kids from various other groups in the woods, come together for a final day that focuses on transition and closure. Just like admission, graduation is a rolling process, so not everyone from the individual groups graduates at the same time. When the teen leaves their individual group, this can be extremely hard and very emotional as the teen says goodbye to their safe people and place—a place where they may have made some awfully hard and important life decisions. More often than not, the teen is scared and nervous and does not want to leave.

While my teen was in this final group of peers, the parents of the graduates attended an all-day parent workshop that helped us plan for the upcoming transition. The staff from the wilderness treatment center used this time to review the skills taught to the teens. They also were able to coach us, parents, through potential situations that could occur at the reunion. Keep in mind that the only communication that has taken place between the parent and the teen was hand-written letters the entire time they were in the woods.

On day two, parents were reunited with their teen for what can be a very emotional and nerve-wracking reunion. I remember being both excited and scared wondering if my teen even wanted to see me. The staff did an amazing job helping families get reacquainted with each other based on the new skills learned and boundaries set during their time in therapy. Once reunited, the teens demonstrated the outdoor skills they had learned including fire setting, fort building, and trap setting. They also shared how these outdoor skills translate to emotional skills and what that means for day-to-day living and coping.

Showcasing these skills helps the trust-building between the parent and teen. Then the parents had the opportunity to practice their teens' newfound skills as their teen coached and supported them. Day two also included a hike, meal, and group-building activities for all the families together. This experience allowed the parents to glimpse what their teen had not only endured, but also how it helped them grow and heal.

Day two ended with the Family Solo when each family had time to be by themselves for a time of sharing and bonding without the distractions of home and outside interferences. Each teen's therapist had a session with the teen and parent to help with this transition. The teens prepared the evening meal for their parents to again demonstrate their meals on the trail as well as to model giving back to the family unit. They were responsible to make a fire for their parents that was used for warmth throughout the night as well as for cooking the meal. This was a vitally important part of the graduation program as it symbolized and demonstrated so much. During this time when the teen gives back to their families, they realize a sense of the mission where service, sacrifice, and the giving of self are profoundly important. These are hallmarks of the wilderness therapy program and ideals.

Although this can be a unique and profound time for families, it can also be tense and stressful as previous behaviors tend to reappear. The new skills and behavior can be a bit uncomfortable and even seem awkward and unnatural. As part of the process, parents and teens were encouraged to begin practicing the new skills and behaviors while under the guidance of the staff at the wilderness programs. All of these behaviors, skills, and challenges would then be discussed during the final session with the teen's individual therapist, which happens the last night before bedtime.

On the night of day two, I sat with my daughter by the fire that she built, as she shared her letter of accountability and confessed the many things she had done before coming to the woods. So much of what I learned that she had done pre-woods, only affirmed that sending her to the woods was the exact right thing to do. Although it was difficult to hear that she had done so much more than I even knew (dropped acid, cocaine, college parties, took my car at night when I was sleeping, and so much more), I was so proud of her for taking accountabilities for all that she had done and coming clean. It was a very emotional time, but more importantly, a time of healing and reconnection.

At the end of the night, we slept in the woods to experience what it was like to go without modern comforts and to really focus on the person in front of me with no distractions and to just be present with each other. She had been in the woods for 79 days. I had never gone that long without seeing or communicating with my daughter. To be beside her in the woods, and hear her breathing, knowing she was healthy, clean, and sober, was the most incredible and overwhelming feeling I have ever experienced. It was a true gift and a true miracle.

Waking up beside my teen on the third day was a special and unique feeling. The range of emotions for both the parent and the teen can cause both excitement and tension all mixed up together. My daughter was actually sad; she did not want to leave. She felt like she was finally able to be herself with no judgment while in the woods. She had committed to her sobriety while in the woods and was worried about staying sober once she left. There is a level of security in the woods that she had not felt in a long time. She did not know what to expect once she left and the not knowing was scary. This was also the first time she had truly authentic relationships and she feared what was going to happen when she no longer had these people with her. It was still tense between us as well, which also made things uncomfortable. Leaving the woods would not be easy, but it was time.

After a quick breakfast and cleaning up of the campsite, the entire group took a short hike to the graduation site. The graduation ceremony honors the accomplishments of each graduate, as well as what they have achieved and realized about themselves. This just may be the greatest thing they have done up to this point in their young lives. During the graduation process, the kids will discuss their journey of healing and growth. Parents also had an incredible journey as well and this is a fun time for them to share with their teens what they have been working on and the growth they have made.

It is there in the woods where the teen, the parent and the family learn, grow and heal; and gain the skills, tools, and knowledge necessary to graduate to the next phase of their lives.

Traditionally, graduation is the successful completion of a course of study in which a degree or diploma is given to students who have successfully completed their program. Graduating from the woods is exactly that, and so much more than that. It is the successful completion of a study of yourself and gaining the knowledge of how to move forward successfully in life. Graduating from time in the woods gives one so much of the things needed in life that we read about in literature. Pythagoras told us to, "Leave the roads and take the trails." Mary Davis said, "I found more answers in the woods than I ever did in the city." And Sir Edmund Hillary let us know that "It's not the mountain we conquer, but ourselves."

THE HOME CONTRACT

Near the end of your teen's time in the woods, some programs have you begin working on a home contract. This will be a collaborative effort between the parent, the teen, and the therapist from the wilderness program. The purpose of this contract is to help both the teen and parent think and plan ahead for the new normal that will now be your home. Ideally, a home contract provides a framework for life at home once your teen has left the woods. This is a critical part of the teen and parent preparing for this transition from the woods to the new structure of the home.

Planning the home contract is one of the first integrated activities that the parent and teen will do together. When the teen knows that they are being heard and able to give insight into the contract they feel like they finally have a voice in the family. It will also show the teen how much they, the parents, have grown as well. Guided by the therapist, this can help deescalate the fears and concerns of coming home by both parties, as well as set boundaries and limits of what the new normal will be. It is an extremely important activity that needs to be taken seriously as planning ahead can help aid in a smooth transition. When a contract is planned ahead of time, it allows for direct and active discussions between the parent and teen with the therapist helping each side state realistic expectations and consequences. Ideally, the contract will include personal insights, improved behaviors, and new values and focus on the key areas in which you and your teen need limits, support, and guidance.

Each contract will look different because every teen is different. The contact needs to be specifically created for the needs at hand, but some key components should be included in every contract. It is important to note that this is not just for the teen. The contract is for all, and the expectation of the parent should also be included. Here are examples of things to address:

-Logistics

-Curfew

-Chores

-School behavior and grades

-Substances

-Cell phone

-Computer and social media

-Use of the car

-Dating/friends

-Attendance at therapy sessions

-Behaviors

-Appropriate expression of anger, violence, and emotions

-How to handle conflict

-Description of the behaviors expected ie: honestly and kindness

-Specific details on consequences and privileges

For me, the home contract was my planning sheet. It was extremely helpful to have this "to do" guide of what needed to happen before my daughter came home. While she was in treatment, I had a lot of peace at my home. I had a fantastic support system that would change significantly once she was no longer in the woods. I knew I still needed this when she came home, but that it would look vastly different. Because recovery is an ongoing process, it was suggested that I create a network that would support my teen, her brother, and myself to ensure that we could be as successful as possible in her recovery. Having this in place ahead of time was a godsend. The suggestions that were made for us, that I would highly recommend are:

-Individual and family therapists for all living in the home

-A parent coach

-Communication with extended family for support as needed

-Individual Support Groups for the teen and parents

-An aftercare program that creates a safe social outlet for your teen

Although a home contract cannot guarantee a smooth transition with no bumps along the way, it can help eliminate some of the worrying, second-guessing, and playing out or the worst-case scenario that can drive you crazy. It will create a framework that can be referred to often as you are learning to live together again. Using the tools that both the parent and teen learn while in the woods can also help with being adaptable to changes that can occur in the contract once they return home. There is no perfect contract that makes everything perfect, but it can lay the groundwork for successfully rebuilding your family. The saying, "failing to plan is planning to fail" could not be more appropriate in this scenario.

EXCERPT FROM LETTER HOME

***Concerning the contract, everything was clear and concise, so there is no room for "I didn't know"*

***Also, even though I may not want everything in the contract I completely understand why it's in there and I respect the fact that it's there*

IMPORTANCE OF AFTERCARE

Once your child comes home it does not mean that all the work is done, and life is going to be great. There is still work that needs to be done. My daughter says that "wilderness got me sober" and the aftercare program "helped me to stay sober." Aftercare has many options and routes to get there. Some people will hire an education consultant to assist them. The consultant will look over your child's file and work with you to decide what the best next option is, and how to get there. For example, some teens will go to a Therapeutic boarding school (TBS), or a residential treatment program (RTC) and the education consultant can help you find the school/program that best fits the needs of your child and family. It was felt that Lucy was not quite ready to come home after her stay in the wilderness program. An educational specialist was hired, and a TBS was found that fit the needs of both Lucy and her family. For Drew, it was felt that he would be able to come home, as long as he continued to work on himself. Since traditional therapy never helped him much he was enrolled in an Intensive Outpatient

Program (IOP). The wilderness therapy program he was at recommended the new program, so we were fortunate that we did not have to hire an education consultant. In the IOP he continued to collaborate with counselors in a group setting with other teens just like him. He participated in this program Monday through Friday for 4 hours a day. As well as going to evening activities 4 nights a week. While this may seem like a lot after spending 68 days in the woods, he has honestly told us that had he not had this aftercare program he would have resorted to his old ways. Like Lucy, he says that wilderness was only the start of his healing.

Some families will choose a discharge plan called "wraparound." This is what it sounds like – the child and family will be wrapped with support and services. A facilitator will work with the family to create their wrap-around team which could consist of extended family members, friends, therapists, and other professionals in the community such as parent coaches and mentors for the child.

Homeward Bound (homewardbound.com) is an organization that offers the teen/family guidance as to the teen's transitions from treatment back into the home. They also offer parent coaching and will function as a go-between between you and your teen's therapist.

Regardless of what path you choose as your aftercare plan, it is especially important to have a solid plan in place for the return home. Unfortunately, I have spoken to some parents who did not have a solid daily plan and their teens regressed from all the skills they had learned.

As parents, we know our children best and we are their best advocates. This is a time to be open and honest with the wilderness program and let them know what you have in mind for aftercare.

WRAP UP

As you begin the journey of navigating all the options surrounding Wilderness therapy we would like to stress that you know your child and family best. You will receive many different views and opinions as to what the best course of action is to take. For example, you will hear that the only way to go is to hire an educational consultant, while someone else will tell you they are a waste of money and advise that you do your own research. We advise that you gather as much information as possible but in the end that you trust yourself and what you feel is the best route for your child and family. As we are proof – there is more than one way to get your child the help that they need.

INDIVIDUAL STORIES

DREW

My son was always a happy goofy child until adolescence hit. Then he became moody, angry, and depressed. He also started to struggle with anxiety. Anxiety often shows itself as anger, and this was true in my son's case. There was lots of yelling, door slamming, and holes in the walls of our house. His grades began to suffer, and he started getting in trouble at school. He went to numerous therapists, but he did not participate in the therapy; therefore, it was never effective. We would have a heart-to-heart conversation with him about his attitude and behavior and he would promise that he would change and do better. We would think this was the time that we had finally gotten through to him, only to experience another outburst the very next day. Our house was tension-filled and we were walking on eggshells, never knowing what would set him off and when the next angry outburst would be.

The day he got suspended from school for the fourth time, he just happened to have an appointment with his counselor. I told the counselor what had happened that day in school, and he asked my son to leave the room. He then sat me down and said that he thought it was time for my son to go somewhere where he could get more intense therapy. This was the first time I ever thought about sending my kid away. The counselor recommended a certain facility and told me to give them a call. When we got home from that appointment, I told my husband what the counselor recommended and his response was, "I was wondering when we'd have to do this." He was not one bit shocked! The next day I called the facility, but they had no availability, so I began researching on my own. A computer search of "wilderness therapy near me" was where I started. This was on a Thursday. After many phone calls to different facilities, by late afternoon Friday, we had selected where he was going. The weekend was spent filling out paperwork, buying the fourteen pairs of underwear on the supply list, and panicking if we were doing the right thing.

Sunday night my husband and I sat our son down and asked him how far he was willing to go to get help. He said he was willing to do anything. So, thankfully, we were able to tell him about the facility we had found, and we did not have to "goon" him. Monday, we went to his school and met with the administration to let them know what we were doing and to see what would happen school-wise for him. They said not to worry, that when he got home, he would have a dedicated teacher who would collaborate with him to get him caught up. Personally, I think they were happy to have him out of the school for a while!

Tuesday and Wednesday were filled with obtaining medical records and my son saying goodbye to his friends. Since he was willing to go away, we did not give him many details as to what to expect when he got there, we were afraid that if he found out too much about the program he might change his mind about going willingly. He says that while he was not "gooned," he was "catfished." He knew he was going but did not know what he was getting! He spent 68 days in the woods, and he still talks about those days with such excitement and pride in what he accomplished. Upon his return from the wilderness, we decided against hiring the educational consultant or sending him to Therapeutic Boarding School (TBS). We found a local program where he would continue to get daily intensive therapy for 12 weeks before transitioning into their aftercare program. This program was filled with other kids just like him—many of who also spent time in the woods.

My son will tell you that wilderness was the best thing for him, and he is so happy he went. He has been out of the program for 2 years and is doing fantastic. He learned to control his anger and how to communicate effectively. We decided to home-school him for his senior year because we felt working on his mental health was more important than putting him back into school where his past could catch up with him and bring him back down. As of 2022 he is 18 years old, has a full-time job, and graduated High School. He is currently working with other troubled kids to help them on their journey to healing. I can honestly say wilderness therapy was life-saving for not only my son but for our entire family.

LUCY

Putting pen to paper for my story proved to be more challenging than I expected it to be. When I think about where we are today versus where we were before wilderness brings up a lot of painful emotions and memories. I am also reminded of how far we have come and how grateful I truly am. I am confident beyond any doubt that going to the woods saved my daughter's life and mine. It put us on a path that was even better than I ever could have imagined.

The dreams we have for our kids and what happens in their lives are often two quite different things. As a parent, I had thought that if I raise kids who are kind-hearted and do good in the world, I would have done an excellent job. I did not expect them nor push them to be extremely high achievers or have so much stress to perform they would break. I gave them time to just be kids. I also encouraged them to be who they were designed to be versus the robot-like Stepford kid that could not be their true selves.

As a child, my daughter always had a bright and funny personality. She was a delight. She was strong-willed and determined but I knew that would do her well in life. She was creative, artistic, and had a great imagination. I appreciated that she was not like everyone else's kid, and I thought that she was comfortable in her own skin. I distinctly remember her pediatrician telling me at her 1-year-old checkup that she had a certain gleam in her eye, and she was going to keep me on my toes – man was he right! One of her preschool teachers told me that she was quite the leader and we joked about if that role was going to be of the free world or the prison riot. Foreshadowing is a funny thing.

I cannot pinpoint the exact moment that I felt like things started to change in her; however, I know she had a very unhappy childhood. She did not grow up in a healthy home. There was a lot of stress in the home. There were also a lot of negative feelings, anger, fear, and mistrust, which ultimately ended in a divorce between her father and me. My daughter has said that she did not care about the divorce and that is not why she started using, but I think it will always be a question in the back of my mind.

My daughter has dealt with anxiety and depression for quite some time. She also has some struggles in her learning style, puts a lot of pressure on herself, and had extraordinarily little self-worth. All this paired with an unhappy home and parents that were not mentally and emotionally healthy led her to long for an escape from dealing with these things. Then the escape turned into full-blown addiction.

She first used drugs in middle school. Like most kids, I believed she was curious. In fact, I fully expected both of my children to try and experiment with things because "that's what teenagers do." Of course, I did not want them to – but I thought it was inevitable. I did not tell either of my kids this because I did not want to give them a "free pass" to try. When

I first found out she had used, I was sad and disappointed and of course, I punished her, saying it was harmful and illegal and I thought it would end there. Little did I know…

She started using in eighth grade. She drank some codeine that a friend gave her when staying after school for a sporting event. By the time she hit her junior year things were unmanageable. She was failing school, kicked off the swim team, and could not be trusted. She tried just about everything with, finally, cocaine being her drug of choice. She lied constantly, manipulated, stole, was really mean, and "used" constantly. I denied and enabled. I overcompensated and begged. I screamed and bargained. I tried each and every one of these things to try to get her to stop. NOTHING WORKED.

Two things happened that led me to the place where I realized that she needed help that I could not give. I realized that I could not simply love her enough to make her better. First was when I received a call from the school telling me that she had missed more than 30 days in just one class, and she was not going to pass her junior year. I was shocked. I had no idea. She had blocked the school's main number from my phone, and I did not receive calls letting me know that she was not in school. Secondly, I learned that she had moved on from pot to dabbing and I was scared. Dabbing is using highly concentrated THC that is in a wax-like substance. It is heated up to create smoke that is inhaled, creating an immediate high. She also used an electric pen (like a vape) called a Dab pen which contained THC. These pens are quite easy to hide and have no smell, so they are being widely used in schools and in homes, with adults having no idea that their child is getting high right in the next room. Most importantly, I have felt it in my gut that if I did not do anything soon, she was going to die. I honestly felt that was my reality.

Her father and I learned about a place in the woods we could send her to help with her addiction. At that point, I had never heard of wilderness therapy, but I trusted the person who recommended it. After briefly looking into it, she was signed up to go to in less than a month's time.

I have shared with many people that this decision was the hardest and most difficult thing I have ever done. I wondered if she would hate me forever and never speak to me again. I was willing to take that risk so she could at least be alive. I will also never forget the day she was taken from my home and how gut-wrenchingly painful that was. However, I knew then and still believe today that it was the single most crucial decision I have ever made, and it SAVED HER LIFE.

After a lot of work and commitment to the process and therapy —for both my daughter and me —I am thrilled to share that in 2022 we celebrated her three-year sobriety anniversary. She also has made the decision to become a wilderness therapist. She is extremely committed, and I have no doubt she will make this happen and be great at it. In her words, she would tell you, "I want to help save someone else's life like the woods saved mine."

At the beginning of this chapter, I said that we all have certain ideas about who our kids would be when they grew up and that as long as my children did good in the world, I would feel like I had done a fantastic job as a parent. Little did I know, the good she is embarking upon will do much better than I ever could have imagined.

SCOTT

I have a different story as I absolutely refused to consider wilderness therapy for almost two years. I mistakenly thought it was cruel and harsh. We wasted so much time and money trying to help our son, and nothing helped. We visited our son at his wilderness program 8 weeks in, and he said "I should have done Wilderness sooner. I hate it here, but I love how I feel." For the first time in many years, he is proud of himself, and you could feel it emanating from him. I am a complete convert and believe Wilderness Therapy helped to change his trajectory.

Our story is long as painful, as many are. Scott struggled with ADHD and anxiety his whole life. He is such a kind and funny kid, charming, and just fun to be around. We did everything we could to help him, working with experts and therapists over the years. Things were dicey in sixth grade when he had behavioral issues that seemed to be growing. We relocated when he was twelve and going into seventh grade. Things really started to spiral at this time. He started vaping nicotine, and then quickly turned to THC. It took me a while to realize what was going on. He is my baby boy; he could not be doing drugs when he is just twelve? Especially, when I am the mom who volunteers in the school and substitute taught! In eighth grade, he was asked to leave his school, and we realized he has a serious drug problem. We found n intensive outpatient program and signed him up for therapy and support—but he was still getting high! He then went to a residential facility for 45 days when he was fourteen. I cried and it felt like it was the end of the world. I had no idea; it would get so much worse from there! He came home and seemed solid! But, 30 days later— we discovered he was still getting high. We then found another residential facility that we sent him to. Sobriety afterward was even briefer, just one week and he was back to getting high, only now he had branched out to other substances too. As I am testing him for typical drugs, he switched to DXM (which is in Mucinex, and other cold medications OTC).

He tried to commit suicide in March of 2020. He almost died. I still feel numb thinking about it. He was having spasms and seizures and doctors did not know what to do to help him. We did not know if it would have permanent mental impairment. I am thankful every day that he recovered. The heart-breaking thing is when we came home—he was still getting high. Now he is fifteen, and we sent him to a THIRD residential facility. It was a wonderful place, he spent 60 days there. It was focusing on trauma, and I thought they were doing good work. Guess what, after two days home—he was still getting high.

So, at this point, I realized something big needs to change. We had spent a boatload of money already and nothing was helping. Not to mention our household was in absolute chaos, and his younger sister was suffering. One therapist told me that Scott needs a "tighter box" and pushed me to Wilderness. EVERYONE pushed me to Wilderness. I sobbed, fought, researched, and worried. I genuinely thought it could break him emotionally. I read the articles that literally make you cry; the articles by young adults who feel like wilderness ruined their lives. I still was not convinced. As I was looking for a fourth residential option two things happened that really changed my mind. The first was, I was afraid he was going to be arrested; we found out that he was trying to steal from the neighbors to get money for drugs. Second, I found pills in his room. I realized if we did not do something DIFFERENT, he was going to die or be in juvenile detention. That was a wake-up for me, that I need to put MY fear and sadness aside and focus on how to save his life. I jumped all in and found someone to help me find the right wilderness program. As I spoke to my educational consultant, he helped assure me that wilderness could work and that a week in the wilderness is like a month at a residential.

After we picked a program, transport came two days later. The nicest "goons" ever came to get Scott at 4 am. He woke up confused and went willingly. He was still high of course!

Now he is at the program, not thriving, but surviving. Scott had said to me many times, "I'm a piece of shit, just give up on me. Why do you care?" At Wilderness, he tried everything he could to get kicked out. He refused to hike (so they did not for a few days), he tried to starve himself (eventually got hungry), and even tried to hit himself in the head with a rock (then got put on watch). Eventually, he realized they were not giving up on him, and neither were we. And, he also realized, I was not coming to rescue him.

The therapists in Wilderness, are like no other. They are healers. Further, the guides are people who give their hearts and souls to these kids. Through this hard journey, we learned what was the core issue with our son. Not drugs—but attachment and self-worth issues. Drugs were a symptom, but not the main problem. Wilderness also promoted family work, which may have saved my marriage. My husband and I were SO far apart, and Wilderness let us see what we were each contributing negatively to each other, and our son.

Scott now sees a future. You can see the confidence in him, he stands taller. And, that good feeling or pride feeds him to want to do more to keep feeling that way. Without getting high! I do not have any delusions that it will be perfect. But I know he has built a solid foundation, and he has a chance. I feel hope for the first time in years.

In 2020, I promised my son I would NEVER send him to Wilderness. I fought it every step of the way, and I was absolutely petrified. In 2021, I felt like I had no other choice, and sent my 15-year-old to the mountains of Utah. It was the best decision I have ever made. I believe it was life-changing for our son and our entire family. I am forever grateful. He is now in a TBS and is continuing the work he started in the woods and is absolutely thriving.

MARK

Our experience with wilderness therapy began when our son was hospitalized for a suicide attempt. He'd struggled for several years with depression, anxiety and just a feeling of emptiness. His father and I always knew something was off and we tried unsuccessfully to fix it with numerous therapist appointments and different prescriptions. His suicide attempt, which we later learned was a cry for help, landed him in the adolescent psychiatric wing of our local hospital for a week's stay. His psychiatrist told us he couldn't come home and needed something more. She put us in touch with an educational consultant, new to us, and that started our wilderness therapy journey.

The educational consultant met with us in her office and saw our son in the hospital to see what program would work best. Her recommendation had a spot available so we started the process of setting up transport and preparing our son. He was mad and wanted to come home. We emphasized the adventurous part of wilderness with hopes it would make him feel better. It didn't. In fact, he used it against us in his first letter home when he accused us of lying about the program. (We later learned this is very typical of the first letter.)

I was nervous about hiring transport but our EC recommended it as a stress-free way to ensure he arrived at the program. He left willingly from the hospital with the transport crew and traveled easily. One of the transport guys let us talk to him on the drive from the airport to the wilderness program. That was a nice gesture that gave us confidence he'd be okay.

The first few weeks were hard as he settled in. He was put on "suicide watch" and was closely monitored in the wilderness. The first set of photos we received showed an angry, tired, and depressed teen. He wasn't happy and we could tell. What kept us going was knowing he was safe.

His first letter home was accusatory and mean. We were prepared for this thanks to our EC but it was still hard to read. Our therapist explained this was typical and to be patient. We were sad and missing our son but we listened to the therapist.

After a few weeks, things started to change. In his second letter home, he apologized for the first letter. And about a month in, we saw our first smiling photo. Our son finally looked relaxed and settled in. He appeared to have friends in his group and was even laughing in one photo. That didn't mean he wasn't having trouble in the program. There were good days and bad days for our son and for me and my husband. Part of his therapy included my husband and I working on our parenting issues. We were slowly learning the part we played in our son's problems. That part was huge.

We followed the program and therapist's recommendations. The letters we exchanged were nice but not mind-blowing. I know some parents receive beautiful letters written by their teens as they progress through the program, letters that display a definite understanding of why they were sent to wilderness. The letters from our son were more basic. And we knew some of what he was writing was simply to follow the "assignment." That was okay. We'd spent several years in a strained relationship with our son that

involved manipulation, misunderstanding, extreme anxiety, lots of frustration, unneeded prescriptions, and exhaustion. We knew wilderness wasn't a quick fix and we knew our son would only do what was needed to "play the game." But he was in a safe place, away from the stressors of every day life, and able to start the process of healing. Wilderness was the beginning of a long process by providing that "reset" in life we knew we were unable to give him at home.

As our son neared the 3-month mark in wilderness, it was decided additional work was needed and so a residential program was recommended. He didn't want to go but knew it was a possibility after talking to other boys in his group. With our son's input, we picked the best program for him and he settled into the idea. He knew and accepted that he needed more work.

I spent the last night of his wilderness experience with him in the desert. I highly recommend doing this if you have the opportunity. It helped me see what the boys go through and to witness the strong bond he created with the other members of his group. I was teary-eyed as they said their good-byes.

I know my son has mixed feelings about his time in wilderness. It was hard and he was in a dark place when he arrived. He has no interest in returning to the area but he does have an understanding of why he needed to go. I think, in time, he'll be thankful. He does sometimes talk fondly about the little things - the inside jokes he had with the other boys, the food they ate and weird recipes they created, and the long, strenuous hikes. Those are the moments I sit quietly and listen, knowing we made the right decision in choosing wilderness.

So here are a few tips for anyone starting this journey.

Tips:

1. The first letter home will be a tough one. Your child is

angry. They're desperate for any sliver of control and will try to achieve it by playing on your emotions. In the past, manipulation has worked in their favor. Try to read through the lines of their letter before you fall apart. And if you do fall apart, that's okay, too. They'll beg to come home, apologize for everything, promise things will be different and on and on. Stay firm and remember why you chose this route. You weren't able to fix the situation at home and needed help to save your child.

2. Parents...work on yourselves. This is huge. Once you realize how much your behavior and parenting affects your child's behavior, real healing can finally begin.

3. Be prepared for the therapist to recommend additional care following wilderness. But also understand, it's not required. Be open to the recommendation. And if your child comes home directly from wilderness, continue working on your mental health and theirs with therapist visits and setting boundaries.

4. While your child is at wilderness, work on yourself. Wait! Didn't I mention this already? Yes! But this part is SO important. There are great books and podcasts about how to parent a child with mental health issues. It's incredibly important to learn how to respond to a child whose anger is escalating and how not to be manipulated by a teen who won't follow boundaries. Plus, looking back at your own behavior can be life-changing. Something as simple as that glass of wine (or three) you drink to calm nerves from dealing with a teen in crisis could be affecting how you react. Taking a hard look at yourself will only improve the relationship with your child.

5. And finally, remember - you're not in this alone. There are so many parents going through the same thing. Reach out and share your story. Find your "people." They're the ones who you can confide in and cry with even if it's virtually. There's something so therapeutic about meeting others who are going through the same stage in life. You've got this.

SAMPLE CONTRACT

Non-Negotiable

Maintain sober lifestyle

-no drugs, alcohol, or nicotine

2) Full participation in an aftercare program

3) School is a priority

-Maintain at least a C average in all subjects

-Be present and mindful during class

4) Be respectful in the way you speak and act

-Treat your mother with respect and let her speak without interruption or dismissive attitude

-Treat everyone's property with respect including the house

*No breaking things or putting holes in the wall

5) No isolating from family

6) Conflict resolution conducted in accordance with skills learned in Wilderness and your aftercare program

7) Honestly in all matters

8) All texts or calls from parents must be promptly answered

9) GPS tracking must always be enabled

10) Answer questions about your day with more than one syllable

11) Sunday nights are reserved for family dinner including conversations about the week's activities

12) Chores and other household maintenance requests will be completed immediately upon request

Negotiable

No media until outpatient therapy is completed, then no more than 2 hours per day

-This includes YouTube, Instagram, Snapchat, or any other social media sites

2) Use of streaming services must be on a TV in the living or loft

3) Phone privileges dependent on the maintenance of non-negotiable and primarily used for communicating with kids in outpatient therapy

4) No contact with old school friends until after outpatient therapy is completed, and then only with approval on a case-by-case basis

5) Employment after completion of outpatient therapy and with approval

Consequences

Non-Negotiable items 1-2

Loss of all privileges for 2 weeks

Non-Negotiable items related to school, behavior, and conflict resolution

Loss of phone and car privileges for 2 weeks with the addition of a 10 pm curfew for 2 weeks

All other items consequences are cumulative

First time: loss of phone privileges

Second time: loss of friends privileges

Third time: loss of car privileges

Addendum

-When negotiating each side will have the opportunity to state their case and provide supporting arguments. You will be permitted no more than three arguments with which to support your claim and will abide by whatever the final decision is without further argument or inappropriate behavior or attitude.

Rewards (Assumes maintenance of all non-negotiable and negotiable items)

Contract will be eligible for review at the completion of outpatient therapy and then every 30 days

Stipend of $40 per week for gas and personal maintenance

Parents will be responsible for car insurance and regular maintenance until you are able to be employed

Senior family trip scheduled for senior year. Activity and location are your choices

5) Family weekend outing of your choice – 1 per quarter

RESOURCES

PALS (parents of addicted loved ones): www.palgroup.org

AA (alcoholic anonymous): www.aa.org

Psychology Today (resource for finding therapist and facilities): www.psychology today.com

Commission on Accreditation of Rehabilitation Facilities (resource): carf.org

Outdoor Behavioral Health Council (resource): obhcouncil.com

National Association of Therapeutic Schools and Programs (treatment resource): NATSAP.org

Evoke Therapy Program (podcasts on mental health): evoketherapy.com

All Kinds of Therapy (research and articles): allkindsoftherapy.com

Find Child & Youth Residential Treatment (treatment & financial resource): childresidentialtreatment.com/category/find-treatment/

Stories from the Field (education): storiesfromthefield.com

National Alliance on Mental Illness (resource/support): nami.org

Sky's the Limit Fund (financial support): skysthelimitfund.org

Saving teens (financial support): savingteens.org

Jason William Hunt Foundation (financial support): jwhf.org

Loa fund (financial support): loafund.com

Parker Bounds Johnson Foundation (financial support): Pbjf.org

Charles N Miller Scholarship (financial support): Charlesnmillerscholarship.com

Homeward Bound (support): homewardbound.com

Success stories (support): ThrivingNow.me

Other parents like me (support): oplm.com

Chose mental health (support): choosementalhealth.org

Right Direction Crisis Intervention (transport): www.rdas.net/

Carrie Blum (education consultant): 984-232-3002

The Pines at Willing Way (treatment facility in GA): wwwv.willingway.com

Clear Fork Academy (treatment facility in TX):

www.clearforkacademy.com

Turnbridge (treatment facility in CT): www.turnbridge.com

Family First (treatment facility in FL): www.familyfirstas.com

SUWS of the Carolinas (treatment facility in NC): www.suwscarolinas.com

Foothills (treatment facility in NC): www.foothillsatredoak.com

Newport: (treatment facility in CA, WA, UT, CT, VA,): www.newportacademy.com

Fellowship Hall (treatment facility in NC): www.fellowshiphall.com

Blue Ridge Mountain Recovery: (treatment facility in GA): www.blueridgemountainrecovery.com

ARCH Academy (treatment facility in TN): www.arch.org

Open Sky (treatment facility in CO): openskywilderness.com

Evoke (treatment facility in UT): evoketherapy.com

Insight (outpatient & inpatient therapy in NC, GA):

www.theinsightprogram.com

**We do NOT have personal experience with all of the above and have done no research into their programs therefore we are unable to endorse any of the above facilities or resources. In our journey, we have met people who have used them and recommended them.

CITATIONS

All Kinds of Therapy. "9 Outdated Half-Truths about the Troubled Teen Industry." All Kinds of Therapy, 17 July 2020, https://www.allkindsoftherapy.com/.

Davis, Mary. "Quote: 'I Found More Answers in the Woods than I Ever Found in the City.'"

Gass, Mike. "UNH Research Finds Wilderness Therapy More Effective and Less Expensive." UNH Today, 23 Sept. 2019, https://www.unh.edu/unhtoday/news/release/2019/09/24/unh-research-finds-wilderness-therapy-more-effective-and-less-expensive.

Guido, Dayna, and Jim Guido. The Parental Tool Box for Parents & Clinicians. Global Heart Books, 2018.

Hillary, Edmund. "Quote: 'It's Not the Mountain We Conquer, but Ourselves.'"

Jenner, Monica. "How Wilderness Therapy Helps with Depression." Medium.com, 12 June 2017.

Louv, Richard. Last Child in the Woods: Saving Our Children from Nature-Deficit Disorder. Atlantic Books, 2013.

Pozatek, Kristine. The Parallel Process: Growing alongside Your Adolescent or Young Adult Child in Treatment. Lantern Books, 2011.

Pythagoras. "Quote: 'Leave the Roads and Take the Trails.'"

Reedy, Brad. "How Wilderness Therapy Works Episode 111." Soundcloud, An Evoke Therapy Podcast, 29 Mar. 2017.

W., Bill, and Bob Smith. "Page 86." Alcoholics Anonymous: The Big Book, Must Have Books, Victoria, British Colombia, 2021.

Wilder, Jenney, and All Kinds of Therapy. "12 Ways Teen Treatment Has Changed since Paris Hilton Went to CEDU." All Kinds of Therapy, 27 Aug. 2020, https://www.allkindsoftherapy.com/.

ACKNOWLEDGEMENTS

To our Tribe – Thank you for all the love and support that you have offered. We are so grateful to have you all in our lives.

To the wilderness therapy professionals who took the time to answer our questions — Thank you for your expertise and willingness to share your thoughts.

To the other wilderness kids and families – Thank you for sharing your thoughts and experiences.

To Maribeth Jenkins — Thank you for doing our final edits.

To James – Thank you for being my rock and keeping me grounded during some crazy times. Love you!

To Sam – Thank you for being so understanding in everything. Love you!

To Kim – Thank you for the technical help, couldn't have done it without you. Hugs!

To my father, David Prince– you are my rock. Many people think they have the best dad in the world… I KNOW that I do. I love you more than I know how to describe, and I can't explain how grateful I am to have your love and support, and wisdom through this journey with Lucy and every single day of my life.

To Jill and Deanna – you are the sisters I got to choose. Thank you for your prayers, always answering the 3 am phone calls, laughter, tears, and your unconditional love and support you have always given and continue to show for me and my daughter. No better friends ever existed! "… to the grave"

To Ann - your understanding and encouragement through this journey based on your knowledge and experiences made a horrible time so much better. You have been an unexpected friend that I love dearly. Thank you for opening both your home and your heart to me and my children; and for praying for us daily… "thumbs up"

To Preston – I know it hasn't been easy for you – that hasn't gone unnoticed. Your resiliency and trust in the process and me have been amazing. I love you more than you will ever know – I am so blessed to be your mom.

Front cover picture courtesy of Tracey E

Made in the USA
Monee, IL
01 November 2022

16951774R00066